PULLING TOGETHER

The 17 Principles of Effective Teamwork

BY JOHN MURPHY

Graphics by Balance Design

TEAM

Teamwork is a "principle-based" value. In other words, if you value teamwork, you have to commit to the principles that grow it. You have to sow the right seeds. To build a healthy team, you have to create an extraordinary amount of faith and belief among team members, a mind-set that puts the team first.

The purpose of this book is to clearly define and explain the 17 "principles" of effective teamwork. These principles serve as the "fundamental truths" leading to synergistic results.

They are constants, non-negotiable laws designed to cultivate trust and foster unity among

WORK

team members. Each is vital to the health and well-being of the team. None can be violated without violating the team.

Use the 17 principles to:

> Build more focus, unity, trust and credibility into your organization.

> Clarify expectations and guide your team on its mission.

> Align your people and your systems, generating more accountability and responsibility among team members.

> Pull together and experience the extraordinary power of teamwork.

THERE IS NO LIMIT TO WHAT CAN BE ACCOMPLISHED IF IT DOESN'T MATTER WHO GETS THE CREDIT.

Principle #1

PUT THE TEAM FIRST

At the center of every high performance team is a common purpose, a mission that rises above and beyond each of the individual team members. To be successful, the team's interests and needs come first. This requires "we-opic" vision ("What's in it for we"), a challenging step up from the common "me-opic" mind-set.

Effective team players understand that personal issues and personality differences are secondary to team demands. This does not mean abandoning who you are or giving up your individuality. It means sharing your strengths and differences to move the team forward. It is this "we-opic" focus that builds trust and creates synergy – the power of teamwork.

To embrace this principle, make sure your team purpose and priorities are clear. What is your overall mission? What is your gameplan? What is expected of each team member? How can each member contribute most effectively? What constants will hold the team together? Then stop and ask yourself, are you putting the team first?

THE WORD COMMUNICATION COMES FROM THE LATIN COMMUNICO, WHICH MEANS TO SHARE.

Principle #2

SHARE TEAM INFORMATION OPENLY

Can you imagine competing in an athletic contest without open access to the score, the clock, and the playbook? How about competing in battle without clear tactical plans and timely communication? Looking to buy a product or commission a service? How informed are the people you are considering?

Without factual information and timely feedback, teams quickly dissolve into weak, dependent groups, shifting responsibility and ownership to those who are informed. In many organizations, this results in a crippling "dependency syndrome," an upward delegation of problem-solving and conflict resolution. Got a problem? Give it to the boss to solve!

High performance teams are empowered teams and information is a source of great power. With it, people can take ownership and act responsibly. Without it, people are captive. To empower a team, begin by sharing information. What are the key metrics and performance indicators for your team? What do you need to know on a daily, weekly, and monthly basis to manage your team performance? Do you know the score?

IF WE DID ALL THE THINGS WE ARE CAPABLE OF, WE WOULD LITERALLY ASTOUND OURSELVES. Thomas Edison

Principle #3

BE PART OF THE SOLUTION

Wanted: High performance team members; passive observers need not apply. Want to be part of a winning team? Get involved. Be part of the solution, not the problem. Speak up. Share your ideas. Put the "we" in front of the "me." Volunteer your time and talents. Effective teamwork means total commitment and participation from every team member. There is no room for dead weight. Every player has an obligation to contribute, to carry part of the load. Without this commitment, a vital bond is broken. Team members have to know they can count on one another.

Effective teamwork requires that everyone leads and everyone follows from time to time, creating a powerful dynamic that invites proactive leadership. We lead when we have something important to say or contribute, using persuasion and influence to benefit the team. We follow when others are leading or when we have a plan in place. What part of the load are you carrying? What special gifts, talents and competencies are you offering? To what extent are you leading and following effectively? What is your contribution? Remember, you don't need permission to be a team player.

APPRECIATION IS A WONDER-
FUL THING; IT MAKES WHAT
IS EXCELLENT IN OTHERS
BELONG TO US AS WELL. Voltaire

Principle #4

SEEK FIRST TO UNDERSTAND

Socrates once claimed, "You have two ears and one mouth. Use them proportionately." How well do you listen? And when you are listening, to what extent are you empathizing, seeking to feel what the speaker is feeling? How well do you really understand your teammates? And how well do they understand you? Are you listening to one another with empathy? Are you communicating effectively? Do you have an honest, open, trusting relationship, nurtured by empathetic communication?

Effective team members recognize and appreciate the power of empathy as a vital leadership skill. They understand that influencing and motivating others, without using authority, requires understanding, perception and respect. To inspire people, we need to tune in to what motivates them. To avoid and resolve conflict, we need to understand what annoys them. To align team members effectively, we need to assess their skills accurately. To relate with people, we need to demonstrate that we understand them.

Healthy partnerships achieve a level of understanding beyond the norm, an almost uncanny ability to intuitively "read" one another's minds. Are you going beyond the norm? Are you connecting with your teammates? Are you listening twice as much as you speak?

A MAN'S MIND STRETCHED TO A NEW IDEA NEVER GOES BACK TO ITS ORIGINAL DIMENSIONS.

Oliver Wendell Holmes

Principle #5

RESPECT OTHER OPINIONS

Synergy grows out of diversity. By bringing people together and encouraging a free exchange of ideas and feelings, we enrich the decision-making process. We gain insight. We get the facts. We identify options. We create alternatives. We challenge the underlying assumptions and perceptions driving individual behavior. We learn about feelings, interpretations and motives. We provide checks and balances to one another, pooling our resources, experiences and competencies to generate more powerful results. The secret to developing win/win solutions is to listen to the people closest to the problem, recognizing that their honest inputs and insights are vital to team effectiveness.

Assess your work environment. Are you encouraged to freely express your ideas and feelings? Do you have a say in important decisions that impact your job? Do you take advantage of this? Do you speak your mind? When you disagree, are your perceptions taken seriously? Do you insist on the same principle with the people you work with? Do you value their inputs? Do you welcome different opinions? Do you consider debate healthy? Do you agree to disagree without becoming disagreeable? Are you using diversity to your advantage?

THE IMPORTANT THING IS NOT TO STOP QUESTIONING. CURIOSITY HAS ITS OWN REASON FOR EXISTING. Albert Einstein

Principle #6

ASK AND ENCOURAGE QUESTIONS

Questions open our minds to continuous learning and unlimited discovery. By asking questions, we identify needs and expectations. We solicit feedback on performance. We learn about competition. We uncover root causes driving results, good and bad. We discover opportunity for improvement. We tap into resources. We foster deeper understanding and healthier relationships.

Building a high performance team requires a healthy level of questioning. For example, what is the team's mission? What is the team's vision? What are the team's critical performance indicators? What information needs to be shared? Who is on board? Who isn't on board? Why? What are the facts? What are the forces against the team? What is our plan to overcome these forces? What other options do we have? What are the advantages and disadvantages for each option? What is our timeline? What resources do we need? How is the team doing? What changes do we need to make? When? Who will champion these changes? What do our customers really think of us? What do our employees really think of us? Do we have our priorities straight? What really matters? Are we asking the right questions?

THE SIGNIFICANT PROBLEMS WE FACE CANNOT BE SOLVED AT THE SAME LEVEL OF THINK-ING WE WERE AT WHEN WE CREATED THEM. Albert Einstein

Principle #7

MAKE RATIONAL DECISIONS

Your team's mission is clear. So is the deadline. You begin meeting to formulate a plan. Before long, the team is at an impasse. Reaching consensus seems way out of reach. Win/win? Not today. You decide to take a vote, splitting the team into winners and losers. The majority rules. Synergy is lost. Feelings are hurt. Your perception of teamwork turns sour. You wonder what went wrong.

High performance teams use a rational process when making decisions and solving problems. This means beginning by gathering data, reviewing the facts and clearly defining the problem. From here, the team gathers ideas, explores options and identifies alternatives. These are "collecting steps," bonding the team together by withholding judgement.

Only when the team has clearly defined the situation, clarified its objectives, and created multiple options does judgement begin. When judging, effective teams use logic and human impact analysis to make a decision, carefully weighing the pros and cons of each option. This "rational" sequence guides the team through important steps, leading to synergistic results. Are you using a rational process when you make decisions?

GREAT DISCOVERIES AND ACHIEVEMENTS INVARIABLY INVOLVE THE COOPERATION OF MANY MINDS. Alexander Graham Bell

Principle #8

ELIMINATE INTERNAL COMPETITION

Cooperating means working together for mutual gain. It means sharing responsibility for success and failure and covering for one another on a moment's notice. It does not mean competing with one another at the team's expense, withholding important data to be "one up" on your peers, or submitting to "groupthink" by "going along so as not to make waves."

High performance teams recognize that it takes a joint effort to synergize, to generate power above and beyond the collected individuals. It is with this spirit of cooperation that effective teams learn to capitalize on individual strengths and offset individual weaknesses, using diversity as an advantage.

Effective teams also understand the importance of establishing cooperative systems, structures, incentives and rewards. We get what we inspect, not what we expect. Think about it. Do you have team job descriptions, team performance reviews, and team reward systems? Do you recognize people by pitting them against standards of excellence, or one another? What are you doing to cultivate a cooperative environment in this competitive, "me-opic" world?

THINGS WHICH MATTER MOST MUST NEVER BE AT THE MERCY OF THINGS WHICH MATTER LEAST. Goethe

Principle #9

BUILD TRUST WITH INTEGRITY

The greatest competitive advantages in life are those that are most difficult to copy. Anyone can put together a group of people and call them a team. Moving furniture around to co-locate people is easy. Buying equipment is even easier. Writing a mission statement? No big deal. Sharing information? In this day and age, we may be sharing too much! And if not, it's an easy fix – certainly not a sustainable competitive advantage.

Now, how do we get people to trust one another? Or cover for one another? How do we get them to be honest with one another? Or even learn from one another? How do we get them to put the team first? These are not quick fixes or problems we can solve with a checkbook. These are challenges that take time and require a total commitment from the leadership.

Trust is a learned behavior, as is distrust, and it is a direct reflection of the team leader. If you do not have trust growing in your organization, start by looking in the mirror. Are you modeling trust and integrity? Are you trustworthy? Are you covering for your team members? Are you honest with your team? Are you learning from your team members and are they learning from you? Are you putting the team first? What kind of role model are you?

WHAT LIES BEHIND US AND WHAT LIES BEFORE US ARE TINY MATTERS COMPARED TO WHAT LIES WITHIN US.

Oliver Wendell Holmes

Principle #10

TREAT ONE ANOTHER WITH DIGNITY

To nurture a healthy, respectful, interdependent culture, team members need to treat one another like winners – with dignity and respect. This means showing up on time, paying attention, asking for and providing help, offering encouragement and support, valuing diversity, and viewing one another as important to the team. Effective team players know that achieving peak performance requires positive attitudes and beliefs on everyone's part. Sustaining peak performance requires dignity and grace.

In order for people to effectively put the "we" in front of the "me," they need to feel confident that the "me" matters. They need to feel good about who they are and what they can offer. This requires a healthy degree of self-respect and self-esteem, a genuine belief that one adds value to the team.

Teamwork is not a dependent process where people abandon the "me" and cling to the team for identity and support. Nor is it an independent process where the "me" comes first. Teamwork is an interdependent process where people rise to a level of sharing, giving and going beyond oneself. Are you cultivating a winning mind-set? Are you looking for the winner in your teammates? Are they seeing a winner in you?

WE ARE WHAT WE REPEATEDLY DO. EXCELLENCE, THEN, IS NOT AN ACT, BUT A HABIT. Aristotle

Principle #11

COMMIT TO EXCELLENCE

One of the most vital bonds holding high performance teams together is a common commitment to excellence – a united quest for on-going improvement. Every player recognizes the need for raising the standards and setting new records. The marketplace does not relax. The competition is not going to let up. Customer expectations will not diminish. The glory days in the past will not protect us in the future. Tomorrow brings with it a new challenge, an opportunity to excel beyond today.

Remember that it is this perception that creates a vital link between team members, especially during times of adversity and loss. Each member must recognize a genuine commitment from one another, making mistakes more tolerable and burdens easier to carry. Committing to excellence means sharing the risk required in generating maximum returns and pursuing victory together.

When you look in the mirror, do you see a person committed to excellence, a tenacious team member striving for total quality? Do your teammates honestly believe you are giving everything you can? Do they see you putting your heart and soul into your work? Do they see you showing up early, staying late, and doing everything you can to improve yourself?

EXAMPLE IS NOT THE MAIN THING INFLUENCING OTHERS – IT IS THE ONLY THING. A. Schweitzer

Principle #12

BE ACCOUNTABLE FOR YOUR ACTIONS

There is no substitute for personal ownership, responsibility and self-control. Accountability breeds quality and empowerment. When we take ownership for a problem and accept responsibility for our outcomes, we become agents of change as opposed to victims of change. When we resist the temptation to blame others or make excuses, we become part of the solution, not the problem.

High performance teamwork requires self-management and self-discipline. Along with goal clarity and role clarity, effective team members understand the responsibility they each have to manage their behavior in line with team principles. This means putting the team first, sharing information, getting involved. When everyone on the team is accountable, the team's effectiveness rises above the sum of its parts. Each team member does not just do what is asked, but what is needed. How are you doing in the area of personal ownership? Do you accept responsibility for your outcomes? Are you part of your team's solutions, or problems? Are you accountable for your actions?

OUR GREATEST GLORY IS NOT IN NEVER FAILING, BUT IN RISING UP EVERY TIME WE FAIL. Ralph Waldo Emerson

Principle #13

ACCEPT MISTAKES AND LEARN FROM THEM

Watch a competitive athlete make an honest error in a game and observe how quickly his teammates offer encouragement and support. What's this? Comfort for a mistake? A pat on the back for a mishap? How can this be? People are paid to do things right, not screw things up!

Now examine your own organization. How are errors in your work environment perceived? How are mistakes handled? Are people given support for taking calculated risks and falling short? Or punished? What is the price for learning in your world?

High performance teams view honest mistakes as part of the learning process. Given everyone on the team is committed to excellence, they review what went wrong, why it went wrong, and then focus on what needs to change. They move forward, recognizing that making no mistakes often implies they are not taking enough risk, not stretching far enough, not learning fast enough. Playing it safe does not elevate people to peak performance. We have to dare to get a hit, recognizing that "striking out" is part of the same process. Give it some thought. Are you ready to step up to the plate?

I KNOW OF NO MORE ENCOURAGING FACT THAN THE UNQUESTIONABLE ABILITY OF MAN TO ELEVATE HIS LIFE BY CONSCIOUS ENDEAVOR. Henry David Thoreau

Principle #14

LEARN CONTINUOUSLY

Effective team members understand that there is no limit to what we can learn, and the more we know, the more we can contribute to a team. Want to know more about a subject? Try reading a book, listening to an audio tape, or asking a peer for help. Want to learn a new skill? Enroll yourself in a class or seminar. Want to advance yourself in this Information Age? Get informed. Read the newspaper. Listen to the news. Buy a computer. Subscribe to a magazine. Go to the library.

Continuous learning by team members compliments and facilitates the ability of a team to function effectively. Talk with the experts. Find yourself a mentor or a role model. Benchmark against the best. Ask a lot of questions. Want to be empowered in this day and age? Empower yourself. Think outside your own self-limiting box to expand your knowledge.

Look at the big picture. The only barrier to lifelong learning is you. Reorganize your time to recognize education as a priority. Volunteer to learn new jobs and skills. Tap into a pay-for-knowledge system at work. Get past your own ego and self-imposed restrictions. The resources are all around you. Are you willing to tap into them to continue learning?

BUILD FOR YOUR TEAM A FEELING OF ONENESS, OF DEPENDENCE ON ONE ANOTHER AND OF STRENGTH TO BE DERIVED BY UNITY.

Vincent Lombardi

Principle #15

PROMOTE INTERDEPENDENCE

In the 1970's, the driving force for organizational change was cost. In the 1980's, it was quality. In the 1990's, speed became a critical success factor. Today, customers want things better, faster and cheaper. This challenges organizations to think differently and work more effectively and efficiently, closing the gaps that typically exist between independent, departmentalized functions.

The emphasis now is on process, the combination of multiple, interdependent functions. For many organizations, this means reengineering slow, vertical hierarchies into fast, horizontal, cross-functional units, giving teams ownership and accountability for processes from start to finish. For team members, it means cross-training to learn the entire process, not just a single, functional skill.

Consider the game of basketball, a very fast, dynamic work environment. Notice that all of the players can perform all of the skills, allowing them to cover for one another quickly and spontaneously. Anything less would be costly.

Now look at your own work environment. Are you looking beyond your existing position? Do you understand the overall process you belong to, from start to finish? Every job fits into something larger. Do you see how interdependent you are? Do you understand how your job fits into the big picture?

WE WILL EITHER FIND A WAY,

OR MAKE ONE. Hannibal

Principle #16

BE PATIENT AND PERSEVERE

Like the gardener, the effective team leader recognizes that cultivating teamwork takes time. Pulling up the "roots" before the process has matured is a sure way to confuse people and destroy what has been started. To grow a healthy team, learn to trust the principles of teamwork and allow the process to take its course.

The vital components to teamwork take time to develop and grow – trust, open communication, we-opic vision, healthy self-esteem, dignity, interdependent growth, participation, sharing, cooperation. Even the most effective teams have conflicts arising from tempers, greed, selfishness, fear and insecurity. This is why patience and perseverance are so vitally important.

The healthy team recognizes that people are people. We have off days. We make mistakes. We have doubts. We assume too much. We differ. This is where great teams distinguish themselves from all the rest. They see these differences as advantages, not excuses to give up. They understand that patience and perseverance are great virtues, the mark of extraordinary wisdom and strength. Plant the right seeds, respect the growing process, and behold the power of teamwork. Are you being patient with your teammates? Are you helping them persevere?

WE MUST

CULTIVATE OUR GARDEN. Voltaire

Principle #17

"PULL THE WEEDS"

Life is full of choices. Some people choose to accept and commit to the principles of teamwork. Others do not. Keep in mind, teamwork is a value. Some people value it, honoring the truths that create it. Others reject it, insisting that these principles are not important. Effective team leaders understand that they have an obligation to align each team member responsibly. Anything less destroys the trust, credibility and respect it takes to build an effective team.

Obstacles and "weeds" must be removed in order for efficient growth to take place. A "weed" is someone who refuses to accept these guidelines, choosing instead to behave independently of the team. Weeds make their own rules, undermining team consensus. A weed expects double-standards. A weed refuses to share and participate. A weed shifts responsibility to others and rejects accountability. A weed looks upon these principles as a disruption, as an annoyance to getting a job done.

Don't be fooled. Weeds may seem harmless. They may even blossom from time to time. But a weed cannot be trusted. Beneath the surface, it is doing everything it can to take over your garden. Pull the weeds and give everyone else some room to grow. Think about it – does your team need a little cultivating?

LESSONS

THE G

Consistent application of the 17 principles of effective teamwork ultimately generates trust, respect and power within any team. Conversely, consistent violation of any one principle destroys this bond. While the author of the following is unknown, "Lessons From the Geese" is a powerful illustration from nature of the principles of effective teamwork. As you read about the natural unity that exists among this species remember – this same unity can exist in your organization!

F R O M

E E S E

As geese flap their wings, they create an uplift for the bird following. By flying in a V formation, the whole flock adds 71% greater flying range than if any bird were to fly alone. > *If we share a common direction and a sense of community, we can get where we're going more quickly and easily because we are traveling on the thrust of one another.*

(continued)

Whenever a goose falls out of formation, it suddenly feels the drag and resistance of trying to fly alone, and quickly gets back into formation to take advantage of the lifting power of the bird immediately in front. > *If we have as much sense as geese, we will stay in formation with those who are headed where we want to go, and we will be willing to accept their help as well as give ours to others.*

When the lead goose gets tired, it rotates back into formation and another goose flies at the point position. > *If we take turns doing the hard tasks and sharing leadership as with the geese, we become dependent on each other.*

The geese in formation honk from behind to encourage those up front to keep up their speed. > *If we "honk," we need to make sure it is encouraging.*

When a goose gets sick or wounded or is shot down, two geese drop out of formation and follow it down to help and protect it. They stay with it until it is able to fly again or dies. They then launch out on their own, with another formation or catch up with the flock. > *If we have as much sense as geese, we too will stand by each other in difficult times, as well as when we are strong. Let us all try to fly in formation and remember to drop back to help those who might need it!*

The greatest accomplishments in life are not achieved by individuals alone, but by proactive people pulling together for a common good. Look behind every winner and you will find a great coach. Look out in front of every superstar and you will see a positive role model. Look alongside every great achiever and you will find caring people offering encouragement, support and able assistance.

Rising to this level of interdependent thinking can be challenging and difficult. Looking beyond oneself, asking for help or accepting help can feel risky. But people are not given life to simply take from one another. We are here to give. Our mission in life is to offer our gifts to benefit one another, to create mutual gain. This is called teamwork, a win/win mind-set stemming from a genuine commitment to the 17 principles that allow it to happen.

ABOUT THE AUTHOR

John Murphy is a highly recognized author, speaker and management consultant. Drawing on a diverse collection of team experiences as a corporate manager, consultant, and collegiate quarterback, John has appeared on over 400 radio and television stations and his work has been featured in over 50 newspapers nationwide.

As founder and president of Venture Management Consultants, John specializes in creating high performance work environments. Among the organizations he has provided services to are AT&T, American Express, Allied Signal, Chase, Hilton Hotels, Prudential Securities, the Michigan State Senate, The New York Times, Target Stores and the CIA. Prior to consulting, John served as corporate director of human resources for Paulstra CRC, an international automotive division of Hutchinson SA in Paris, France.

John is a graduate of the University of Notre Dame and the Human Resource Executive Program at the University of Michigan, and now lives in Grand Rapids, Michigan, with his wife, Stephanie, and their four children.

His other books include: *Agent of Change: Leading A Cultural Revolution, Reinvent Yourself: A Lesson In Personal Leadership, Get A Real Life: A Lesson In Personal Empowerment, The Eight Disciplines: An Enticing Look Into Your Personality,* and *Think Change: Adapt and Thrive, or Fall Behind.*

For more information, contact: *Venture Management Consultants, Inc.*
PO Box 6651, Grand Rapids, MI 49516 Phone (800) 942-1120 Fax (616) 942-2122
E-mail: jmurphy@iserv.net

The cost is low... but the ideas are priceless!

Each title in the Successories "Power of One" library takes less than 30 minutes to read, but the wisdom it contains will last a lifetime. Take advantage of volume pricing as you share these insights with all the people who impact your career, your business, your life.

Anatomy of A Leader
This collection of insights written by Carl Mays represents a simple thought-provoking body of knowledge that can help everyone develop the qualities of a leader. #713259

Attitude: Your Internal Compass
Denis Waitley and Boyd Matheson give powerful examples of how a slight shift in the way you see the world can yield powerful results in an ever-changing workplace. #713193

Burn Brightly Without Burning Out
This book, by motivational expert Dick Biggs, will boost morale and productivity by helping people balance the work they do with the life they lead. #716016

Companies Don't Succeed...People Do
Successories founder and Chairman, Mac Anderson, outlines "The Art of Recognition" – how to develop employees and a recognition culture within any organization. #716015

Dare to Soar
The spirit of eagles inspired this unique collection of motivational thoughts by noted speaker Byrd Baggett. Any goal can be reached if you "Dare to Soar." #716006

The Employee Connection
Noted employee motivation expert Jim Harris provides dozens of practical methods for leaders to "unleash the power of their people." #716018

Empowerment
Ken Blanchard and Susan Fowler Woodring's valuable insights into empowerment outlines how to achieve "Peak Performance Through Self-Leadership." #716022

Motivating Today's Employees
Recognition expert Bob Nelson offers a great primer on the impact of employee rewards and recognition. #716007

Motivating Yourself
Mac Anderson, Successories founder and Chairman, offers a mix of proven ideas and motivational thoughts to help "Recharge the Human Battery." #716021

Motivation, Lombardi Style
Use the coach's memorable collection of insights about the athletic playing field and the business battlefield to inspire your team. #716013

Pulling Together
Nationally-noted author and speaker, John Murphy, outlines "17 Principles for Effective Teamwork" with a refreshing mix of information and thought-provoking questions. #716019

Quality, Service, Teamwork
Share these "Foundations of Excellence" with your employees! This valuable resource includes over 100 motivational quotes. #716014

Results
Help your sales team turn passion into profit and maximize their relationship power with these proven strategies for changing times. Jeff Blackman's experience and style makes this an entertaining handbook that guarantees results. #716017

Rule #One
Author and customer service expert C. Leslie Charles has compiled dozens of insightful ideas, common sense tips and easy-to-apply rules in this customer service handbook. #716008

Teamwork
Noted consultant Glenn Parker gives managers, team leaders and members a valuable blueprint for successful team building. Put it to work for your team! #716012

Think Change
This intriguing book, by John Murphy, challenges today's employees to change their thinking to keep up with an evolving workplace. "Adapt and Thrive or Fall Behind." #716020

To order call toll-free 800-535-2773